REMEMBERING DAI
by Nami Nakamura
An Adult Coloring and Activity Book
for Grief, Loss and Comfort

This book is dedicated to and in memory of my dad, Don Kim, who passed away on August 31, 2017. This project began as my way to cope with the tremendous loss of losing my beloved dad. As I interacted with others who have and are experiencing loss, it became clear that this project can be a tool to help others cope with their losses and also give friends and family a way to give a meaningful gift as they reach out to those in the grieving process.

For those of you who have lost your dad, I hope this coloring book will bring a sense of closeness to him, some comfort in your pain, a reminder of his love and a sense of closure as you say goodbye to your beloved dad. Nothing will take away that sense of loss, but I hope you will sense his love and be in touch with the memories that bring you close.

May God bless you on your journey of healing and wholeness.

~Nami Nakamura

Remembering Dad
by Nami Nakamura
©2017 Nami Nakamura

All rights reserved. No part of this publication may be reproduced, distributed or transmitted in any form or by any means, including photocopying, recording or other electronic, mechanical or manual methods without the prior written permission of the author, except in the context of reviews and promotion.

How To Use this Book:

Start where you like and use colors that reflect your emotions, feelings and loss. The lined pages are for you to express written thoughts, feelings and memories. They can be written as a continuous thought, or as lists or phrases that come to mind. The blank pages are there if you would like to add pictures or artwork to personalize this book.

Everyone expresses creativity differently just like everyone expresses grief differently. There is no timetable as to how long you should grieve. The love and depth of emotions goes deep, so it is not something to "get through" but one to "feel through". Allow yourself to feel the love and loss of your dad or father figure. He made a huge impact on you, so lovingly remember his life and let your creative expressions be moments of giving thanks and to say goodbye in your own way and time.

The artwork is designed so you can color in it like other coloring books, but can also be framed to commemorate his life or to give away to others grieving with you. You decide what is best. You can even buy a second book to express other emotions as they come, to continue the grieving process.

Who This Book is for:

This book is for anyone grieving, who needs comfort or is suffering loss or for those you know that lost someone or is losing someone to death, hospice, terminal illness, dementia or mental loss. Grief and loss is a process and takes many forms. Coloring is a personal and peaceful way to reflect and come to terms with it in a loving and gentle way.

Note from the Artist:

The artwork is handrawn and has imperfect and charming qualities that set it apart from commercial and computer generated art. Enjoy the uniqueness of this style as you color and express your love and loss.

Printed in Great Britain
by Amazon